Wounded **VOICES**
Unwise CHOICES
THE TRUTH FROM OUR YOUTH

To. Janae,

My desire and hope
for you is that you'd
be encouraged to do
the best by yourself.

Wiesha

Wounded VOICES
Unwise CHOICES
THE TRUTH FROM OUR YOUTH

MISCHA P. GREEN

MORALS & VALUES PRESS
A Division of Greatness Now!

For information address: Morals & Values Press, 2327 Harlem Avenue, Baltimore, Maryland 21216.

Published by

MORALS & VALUES PRESS
A Division of Greatness Now!

DEDICATION

This book is dedicated to my two sons, Kyle and James; both of whom have made my twenty plus years of parenting such an enriching and enjoyable experience that being neglectful and inattentive has never been an option. In my opinion, our relationships typify the benefits of depositing quality stuff into your children.

Also to my nieces—Erin and Mischa, as well as my nephews—Taj and Eean; as each of you already know, I am tickled pink to be the aunt of four of the craziest, yet most gifted young people in the world. Continue to connect with your gifts and God will continue to make room for them.

And finally, to the innumerable youth who over the last twenty years have accepted my love and permitted me beyond the veil to the innermost parts of your fears, joys, hurts, and struggles. This book is for you. I heard you then and I am still listening now. Better am I from having known you.

CONTENTS

Listen! Do you hear that? I believe its voices. Can you hear them? They sound like the voices of some youth who are perhaps attempting to get our attention. Can you hear them? Some of the voices are gravely muffled as they must resonate through anger and bitterness and fear. Other voices are loud and boisterous as they intrusively resound from the platform of deviant and delinquent behavior. Still other voices are unnervingly quiet as it hurts too bad to think about the betrayals, much less attempt to articulate how much the betrayals hurt. Yet if we listen close enough, out of the belly of silence a concentrated and deliberate message is being spewed.

Regardless of the volume or the method of communication, if we adults do not have an ear to hear and a heart to rescue our youth from destruction's wicked grasp, we will remain conspirators who perpetuate wickedness by throwing our youth back into the mouths of that which seeks only to eat them alive. I ask you how many more of our youth have to drop out of school, abuse drugs, prostitute themselves, be incarcerated, kill someone, or die before we decide to listen? Sorrowfully, everybody is waiting for somebody to become involved, which typically and unfortunately only happens as a result of something catastrophic – like a school shooting, or a community drive-by.

The reality is tragedy should not be the broom upon which we fly onto the "help our troubled youth" scene. We all have an obligation to breathe life into the nostrils of our young people every single day. Parent, preacher, teacher, lawyer, mailman, and sanitation worker alike; we all are preservationist in our own right and must begin – right now – to serve in this capacity.

Wounded Voices Unwise Choices prolifically documents this truth. The six brief stories that are illustrated by the author yet lived everyday by countless youth give us an up close and personal account of both the advantages of investing in our youth, as well as the devastating affects of our turning away from and tuning out our youth.

Although the stories are short in length, they are long in depth. As you read you will notice that there are no names used at all. Know that the absence of names is deliberate and seeks to convey how insignificant names are when we speak about the burdens and baggage our young people shoulder. The relevance, therefore, is in the message that the messengers (our youth) are giving to us.

As you engage in this read may conviction like a ferocious wind sweep through your psyche and compel you to participate in some moments of introspective reasoning relative to your involvement with our youth. May you be driven to a place of deep contemplation as you ponder the following questions: Do you speak kindly to our young people when you encounter them? Do you affirm their worth by correcting them when you see them degrading themselves? Do you model before them who they can be? Are you a walking contradiction, and an embarrassment to those of us who are living accountable lives? Do you in fact have a position where our young peoples' well being is concerned? Are you coaching our youth through the battlefield of their mixed up minds? Or, are you on the frontline funneling through injurious ammunition that immortalizes their demise? Consider as you read where you stand in the preservation of our youth, for they are counting on us you. And they are counting on us to in some instances save them from themselves.

Wounded VOICES
Unwise CHOICES
THE TRUTH FROM OUR YOUTH

Chapter One

Please, those seven bullets I pumped in yo
didn't prove anything but how weak I was.

And I thought shooting him would prove my point. He did need to know who was in charge. I wasn't gonna let him be confused another day about where I stood. So I shot him. Not one time. Not two times. But seven times. *Pop, pop, pop, pop, pop, pop, pop.* I had heard that seven was the number of completion. No doubt I liked the thought of completing a cat who thought respecting me was optional.

But somehow it all went wrong. He took seven hits, but he didn't die like I planned. And not only did he live, he was conscious enough to name me. I did the run thing for a bit, but that got tired quick. Not to mention Five-O was getting too close for comfort. You know scared folk become talking folk. Five-O put the heat on and so as not to cause problems for my peeps, I decided to turn myself in.

Being in here, all locked up ain't what's happening. Don't nobody in here care nothing about me. The guards talk to us like we ain't shit. Niggas and chics treat each other crazy, man. You just another number. You almost forget you got a name cause don't nobody use it. They call you yo, whore, bitch, nigar, stupid, dumb . . . or a number. And to think I'm in here because I wanted respect. Please, those seven bullets I pumped in yo didn't prove nothing but how weak I was, for real.

Now that I don't have time to do anything but think – cause I'm too far for my peeps to visit, and the letters they send I can't really read – I can be real with myself. All that trying to show your boys how tough you think you is ain't where it's at. Laying up in some dude's house chillin', getting blasted, talking smack, when I knew I needed to be in somebody's school was a waste. Some days I did really ask myself what was I doing. What the hell was I thinking? Or, why wasn't I thinking? Plain and simple, I just didn't have the heart to step away. That's really what it boils down to when you think about it.

One day when I was at my P.O.'s (probation officer) office, he told me that punks hide behind guns and violence. He said suckers take what don't belong to them, because they too lazy to go out and work for their own. He was telling me how real men accept the challenge to stand up and do what's right. Like providing for a family, going to work everyday, spending time with your children, going to school to get a decent education so you can make something of yourself.

Although I heard him, I wasn't really trying to listen to that stuff he was talking. On another visit he was telling me how "the system" is set up for our demise – what that word meant I didn't know, and I was too cocky to ask. He said, "They want you all to keep fighting over turf, killing each other over stupid stuff, and standing on the corner when you should be in school. Their hope is that you will stay ignorant and never come to the understanding of your full potential."

Man, I was like, whatever. I was looking at him like he was on something . . . like he was the one getting high. If I wanted a sermon I would have gone to church. All I wanted to do was sign in, take my piss test, and be out. But every time I went to see my P.O. he would feed me that "positive stuff." It was different, though, because everybody else just called me a loser. My family actually told me I was gonna go to jail like my father. My grandmother said I didn't know what "do right" looked like. It made me think, why try. If don't nobody else have no expectations of me why should I have any of myself. It ain't gonna make no difference anyway.

Today, though, while I chill in this ran down facility that ain't fit for animals much less humans, I kinda think that all the stuff my P.O. said was right. I could never figure out or understood why this dude cared about me, but I know he did. I could sense it. No, I didn't know what it was then, but looking back I know what it is now.

I also know if I would've listened to him I probably wouldn't be in here – locked up, confined, being treated like trash. I would have been in school trying to get something in my head. But to be honest, I didn't think it was worth it. Why? Cause I seen people who did it the right way struggle bad. I seen innocent babies be left stranded by their mothers who'd rather chase that crack. I seen hard working, upright people die for no apparent reason.

People like the man down the street. I mean this man worked hard. I would see him go to work everyday. He took care of his wife and kids. On Sunday mornings they never missed going to church. This man was cool. He was quiet. Didn't bother nobody. He spoke to me and my boys every time he saw us, unlike the other grown ups in our block.

One night, though, fire truck sirens lit up our neighborhood. They were coming from everywhere. Me and my boys was in the house getting high and ran outside because all we could smell was smoke. The whole neighborhood was smoked up. We looked up the street and it was that man's house. Flames was coming out. Man, the house was blazing. By the time the fire people got in there it was too late. Out he and his family came in those black bags . . . one at a time. Nobody made it. "What the hell happened?" was all I could say. Later, the word was it was faulty wiring in the house. That thing messed me up, man. I couldn't believe it. Of all the houses in our block, why his house? A God . . . please. There can't be no God. Nobody was more upright than this man. He was handling his business. Though I never made it my business to tell him, I liked that man. I admired what he was about. From a distance I peeped him, and thought to myself, "Only if I had a father like that."

Well, it's a bit late for that now. I'm here, he's gone, and to this day I never understood how God could let something so bad happen to somebody so good. But that's not the only thing that I wonder about. I wonder why, out of all the children in the world, I had to be born with nothing . . . no father . . . no real mother. I wonder why – after all that Martin Luther King and them cats did for us – Black people don't try harder for themselves. Yeah, I sold drugs. I didn't help matters, but I didn't have a choice. My mother needed my help. Selling, I was able to help feed her habit and put food on the table for my sister and brothers. I also wonder why the world see Black men as animals . . . as nothing. I just wonder why things have to be the way they is – bad, and cruel, and sad, and painful.

Even in school, when I did go, them teachers – most of them – didn't care about teaching us nothing. They called us all kinds of names. It was nothing to walk up the hall and hear two teachers talking about a student. And don't think about not understanding something. Wasn't no room for that. Man please, I stopped going to school in the 10th grade and I could just barely read three and four letter words. Some other words I had lucked up and memorized just on the strength of seeing them all the time.

The teachers, they'd call you dumb and stupid. They'd make fun of you. They'd embarrass you. Some would call your mother, that they didn't even know, trifling. Man, I hated school. There was one teacher – my math teacher – who was mad cool, though. She treated us with the utmost respect. But the other teachers even came down on her for being nice to us. She didn't care, though. She could feel where we were. Sometime in her class, she would put the lesson to the side and just go there with us. I would leave her class really thinking she was on our side – sure nuff. We appreciated her and we didn't think about disrespecting her like we did our other teachers, cause she respected us and we gave it back.

In here, what they call school is a joke. The books are so old the pages are yellow. They teach us on a 3rd grade level cause we supposed to be stupid. The teacher said, "I talk to you like the dummies you are, because only dummies go to jail." It's a shame that it took me to actually get here to realize I don't belong here. I am better than this. Despite what my family said, I bet if I put my mind to it I could turn my life around and be the man my P.O. talked about, or be like that man in my neighborhood. I bet if I gave somebody a chance to help me, I could be an example and maybe even get through to my boys back round the way. For real, my life ain't as hopeless as I thought. I got two years to do in here, but I can make this time work for me.

The dude who came in here doesn't have to be the same dude who walks outta here. I'm learning that everything is what you make it. It's time to stop making excuses, and start making plans to make something of myself. Cause when I step up out of here, ain't no coming back, not for the kid. Boys or not, I gotta be smart. I gotta want something more out of life than a blunt, a forty, and some butt. I gotta prove to myself, first, that who my father is is not who I have to be. It ain't about nobody else. It's about me and what I want. My teacher back home used to say, "When you knock at the door of good, God will always have someone there to open it and welcome you to the other side." I guess I'll soon find out.

Chapter Two

Grandmommy used to say,
"Ain't nobody but God gonna tell
you the truth like your conscious."

We were together for three years, from the ninth to the eleventh grade. You would think that by now lies would be a thing of the past. You would think we were beyond keeping secrets. When I told him I loved him I meant it. I also believed he meant it when he told me he loved me. It sounded sincere. It also felt sincere when we had sex. There was no doubt in my mind that it was all about us. Although my girlfriends would tell me they saw him hollering at other chicks from time to time, I'm thinking there's nothing to that. After all he is fine, tall and slender, who wouldn't want to holler at a brother like that. He could hold his own in the schoolhouse, too. Those girls weren't crazy. Like me they knew a good catch when they saw one. I would have been delirious to think that nobody would pull up on him. I more or less figured it was his responsibility to push them back and make them aware that he was spoken for.

Apparently, I was wrong and my girls were right. He was doing more than hollering. He was creeping – big time. And would look me dead in the face and deny it. But like my mother always said, "What's done in the dark will come to the light, sooner or later." I wanted to know, but not the way I ended up finding out.

Being naïve and thinking I could trust him, we stopped using condoms at his request. "Girl, I love you. I wouldn't put either one of our lives in danger. We've been together for a whole year, and if you don't trust me by now then maybe . . ." Before he could finish his statement I was sold. No more condoms. Flesh to flesh it was. Now, I must admit, ain't nothing like the feeling you get when you can feel him and he can feel you. But there was not a time we had sex without a condom that I did not think about my safety. Something in my mind kept telling me I should just take the risk of losing him and tell him I didn't want to do it anymore without a condom. At the same time, though, I was afraid to lose him. I loved him.

Often, I would think about the TV commercials and the safe sex literature I'd read that said stuff like: If he loves you he'll respect your right to protect yourself. Yet I still didn't feel comfortable pushing the issue, but neither did I feel comfortable not pushing the issue. Grandmommy used to say, "Ain't nobody but God gonna tell you the truth like your conscious." Well, I guess she was right. Too bad I didn't have enough courage to listen to my conscious. Two years, several tests, and one life-changing diagnosis later, I could hear my grandmommy saying, "Baby, you should've listened."

Because not only did I contract HIV, which is disgusting in and of itself, but I've brought a child into this world who was fortunate enough, because of the medical advances, to not become infected with HIV, but was not fortunate enough to be numbered among the many children who – of no fault of their own – are forced to grow up without the influence, the love, the support, or the presence of their daddy. I thought I was pretty smart, and so did he. Obviously neither one of us were as smart as we should have been.

I'm sure that by now he knows he's infected with HIV, which is probably why I haven't heard from him. It's as if he just vanished off the face of the earth. Even his family has been acting real cold and strange. This is the same family, by the way, that absolutely adored me once upon a time. There's a part of me that believes he was out there so much that he probably doesn't know where he contracted the virus from. Then there's another part of me that thinks he may have known, and somehow thought he wouldn't pass it on. Either way, if I was him I'd have a hard time facing me too.

Trust me, I'm not trying to justify his disappearance or anything like that. I'm just trying to understand how my life could be turned completely upside down so quickly. I'm trying to figure out what kept me from listening when that inner voice clearly told me to protect myself.

It is not easy having to live with the consequences of your decisions, especially when you had the power and the information to make a better decision. Like him, I felt like running when I realized I had to tell my mother. She and I have always had a great relationship and I appreciate so much how hard she has worked to provide for me and my brother.

The last thing in the world I wanted to do was disappoint her. She has always thought so much of me. What would this do to our relationship? Here she respected my decision to work full time rather than go to college, which is a decision I made solely on being able to be home with "my man". Of course I didn't tell my mother that, though. And she agreed I could live at home as long as I worked and saved my money. How could I pull the rug from under all that? I may not have wanted to, but I had to. I didn't have another choice. My mother has always been honest with me, and she's raised us to always be honest with her. So . . . I told her.

She looked at me. She told me how she felt. And believe it or not, she gave me the same love and support she has since I was born. I know she was hurt. I know she was disappointed. I know she was a lot of other things, too. But despite what she felt, her concern was that I keep my head up and stay strong. She had every right to ask me to pack my bags and leave, but she didn't. Instead, she told me to let go of my anger and bitterness toward my child's father, because I was as irresponsible as he was, and therefore didn't have any right to be any angrier with him than I was with myself.

She lovingly reminded me that I was the one who ignored my conscious. I was the one who opted not to protect my own life. I realized that she was not blaming me as much as she was holding *me* accountable for *my* actions, which is really what it's all about. For my mom, the bottom line was the damage had already been done. In her words, there was no need in crying over spilled milk—especially when I was the one who knocked the glass over. She really wanted me to know that weeping over what I should've or could've done was useless at this point. He did what he did, but he was only able to do it because I gave up control.

I have so much respect for my mother. She remained consistent in demonstrating her love for me and for my new baby. Even on my bad days when the virus was getting the best of me, she was patient and kind. Many days I'd lie in the bed crying because I didn't have the strength to feed my own child and my mother was right there caring for both of us at the same time. Her strength was remarkable. She never complained although I knew it was difficult for her to see me in the condition I was in. She never fussed. She just mothered me and my child without hesitation. And I could feel that she wasn't doing it out of obligation, but out of her love for us.

Do I still think about my child's father? Yes. Do I wonder how he's doing? Yes. Do I wish I had listened to my conscious? Yes. Did I ever think I'd get HIV? No, not really. But I have it and all I can do from here is accept what my reality is, learn something from the choice I made, and maybe help somebody else to not get in the situation I'm in. I really hope my irresponsible choice will help to save somebody else's life even if it doesn't save mine.

Chapter Three

*My pastor told me if I wanted to be
blessed of God, I had to be around people
who had the mind of God.*

When my mother would talk about our pastor I thought he was perfect. Every Sunday he would stand up in the pulpit, and although I could not understand everything that he said all the time, I liked the way it sounded. He preached with power. He knew the Bible like I'd someday like to know it. And what he said he wanted more than anything was for those of us who sat under his teaching to learn how to love and serve God. I guess that's why my mother loved my pastor so much.

One day I told my mother that I had a problem I wanted to talk to my pastor about. I told her I needed him to give me some direction. She immediately encouraged me to make an appointment to see him. I did and he was glad that I came to talk to him. I told him that I hoped he still felt that way after I finished telling him what my problem was. After a word of prayer he instructed me to share. I told my pastor that I was struggling with these thoughts I kept having about other young men. I could not understand why being a young man, I was so strongly attracted to other young men. I had not done anything with anybody. I actually tried to do the girlfriend thing to see if I would like it, and also because my friends and family kept asking me why at fourteen I didn't have a girlfriend yet.

I went on to tell with my pastor that I had people tease me about my feminine tendencies, but I have no control over them. He leaned toward me, put his hand on my hand and said, "Son, it's okay. You are going to be fine. I don't want you to worry about what people say. I don't want you to try to be someone you are not. You just be yourself. I know it took a lot of courage for you to come here today, and I am going to be here for you. I will help you through this."

It was not long after that meeting that my pastor sort of took me under his wing. He became my friend. We did things together. He would permit me to come to his house and eat dinner with him and his family, who was also very welcoming to me. He would pick me up for church on the weekends that my mother had to work. My mother was so happy that our pastor had consented to more or less mentor me. His reaching out to me confirmed for her that he was the great man she always said he was. More than that, I was happy that my pastor promised not to tell my mother about our meeting even without me asking. I almost felt like he could feel my anxiety and shame about possibly being an embarrassment to my mother if she were to find out. Not to mention, my mother is a very religious woman who would have thought I was the devil himself if she ever knew what I was secretly struggling with.

The more I hung around my pastor the more like him I wanted to become. He made me feel real special. I thought that telling him about my attraction to young men was going to make him look down on me or something, but it didn't. It was almost as if he felt sorry for me and decided to help me feel better about myself. We became so close that there was almost nothing we couldn't talk about. Instead of feeling weird, I felt quite comfortable around my pastor. Like my mother, I began to believe he was a great man of God who loved God and God's people.

About a year and a half after my pastor took me under his wing, he asked if I would like to go with him to a father and son retreat that he was invited to speak at. Without hesitating I said yes. I asked my mother and she thought it would be a wonderful growth opportunity for me. She had seen how much I was reading my Bible and wanting to learn more about God so I could be a righteous man like my pastor. She saw how I had stopped being around my old friends. It wasn't that they were bad, it was just that my pastor had told me if I wanted to be blessed of God I needed to be around people who had the mind of God. So that's what I did.

The weekend would come for us to go to the retreat. I was too excited. My mother was excited and my pastor was glad I accepted his invitation. A couple deacons and men from our church drove up with their sons, too. I thought for sure I would be rooming with another young man and my pastor would room by himself, but when we got there and room assignments were given out, he told me I would be rooming with him. At first I wondered if he didn't let me room with another young man because of what I had shared with him, but I tried not to get stuck there. I really wanted to enjoy myself. And enjoy myself I had until the second night. That's when things took a turn I never saw coming.

We had a nice day of teaching and fun. I learned a lot. Some of the other young men and I had a chance to talk about how challenging it is to do the right thing with all the temptation of the streets. We were talking about how it seemed like adults really don't get what we are saying sometimes. We were talking about how we need men to talk to and teach us how to become productive men. On that note I told them how thankful I was for my pastor and how he took me under his wing. The other guys thought I was quite fortunate to be so close to my pastor. After we finished our conversation we all went to our rooms to get a jumpstart on packing.

I got in the room before my pastor and got stuff together because we would be leaving to return home early in the morning. After I packed, I showered, said my prayers and then went to bed. Pastor came in later because he and the men were still talking and sharing. I woke up when I heard him shut the door. He turned on the light and saw I was awake. He apologized for disturbing my rest and asked if I'd had a good weekend. I told him it was great. I told him I had learned a lot, and then I thanked him for bringing me. I told him I would never forget how nice he'd been to me. After we talked a bit he excused himself and went to shower. While he was in the shower I tried to go back to sleep but I couldn't. I don't know if it was the shower water or the TV that pastor had turned on, I just couldn't go back to sleep. So I laid there looking at the ceiling and thinking.

I began to think about how fortunate I was that God put my pastor in my life. I was thinking about how right my mother was about my pastor being a great man who loved God and His people. I thought to myself, "It doesn't get any better than this." Just then my pastor came out of the shower. He had on his robe. He turned the light out and walked over toward my bed. At first I thought that he was coming to say good night, but then I thought he could've said that from his bed. Maybe he's going to pray with me, was my other thought. But that was wishful thinking. The truth is I didn't know what to do or say, I just knew that something – all of a sudden – didn't feel right.

As pastor sat on the edge of my bed, I moved over to put some space between us. Just then pastor put one of his hands on my hand and the other hand on my stomach on top of the cover. I was lying on my back. All of a sudden I got this funny feeling in my gut and a lump in my throat. I felt like I needed to swallow but I could not. He looked at me and said, "Son, how have you been doing?" Nervously I responded, "Fine. I've been doing fine." He said, "How have you been handling your problem?" I said, "Problem, what problem pastor?" He said, "The problem you came to me about a year and a half ago." I said, "Pastor, God has really helped me. I think that reading my Bible, praying, and being around you is really making a difference."

As I was talking, my pastor lifted my hand that he had his hand on and placed it on his leg. He started moving his other hand down my stomach to my lower part. I wanted to scream, but it was almost as if my body became numb. I wanted to ask him what he thought he was doing, but instead I just looked at him. He looked back at me, and before I could say anything, he said, "Son, we are going to be just fine . . . you and me." He said, "I like you. You are a smart boy."

What does he mean by we're going to be just fine, I thought to myself. What is he doing—for God's sake? I wanted to say something, but what. What do I say to a man that's taught me so much. Given me so much. Taken so much time with me. A man that my mother thinks the world of.

Before I knew it, he had untied his robe with nothing under it. Had moved my hand up his leg and onto his private part. I wanted him to stop. I need to stop him, but how?

This was the beginning of a year and a half of agony, shame, and a whole lot of pain. From fifteen and a half to seventeen my pastor made me his lover. He stole from me the very thing I was trying to hold on to. I told nobody. Who would believe me? Certainly not my mother because as my pastor said she would listen to him before she listened to me. I tried to think of who I could go to. I also tried, a number of times, to reject him but he paralyzed me with one threat after another. I tried to turn down other invitations to go out with him, but my mother would chew me out and all but force me in the car. Why me? How could a man of his status do something like this? He had a church, a family, and he knew God did not approve of what he was doing. Confused was not the word for what I had become. I was so messed up that I literally thought I was going to lose my mind.

Not only was he wrong, but he tried to justify it by putting God in it. He told me that God had given me to him. What made bad matters worst was when I found out that he wasn't the only man in our church doing this and I wasn't the only young man being victimized. I wanted to fight. I wanted to go to the police. I even thought about telling his wife, but she's been married to him for 23 years. I've known him for only 3 of them years. What can I say about her husband? She would more than likely think I was up to no good before she would believe something wasn't right about him, especially considering how good they had been to me.

Then, there was my mother. What would this do to her? She was active on all these boards at our church. A lot of people respected and liked her. She and my pastor's family was real close. He had a lot of influence over her . . . her thinking . . . her parenting of me. How could I just disrupt all that? I mean she adored this man. This stuff would rock her world, and jack up her spiritual foundation.

As luck would have it, I graduated high school and chose to go out of state to college—for no other reason than to get away from my pastor. But proximity meant nothing. I was haunted by the memories of his betrayal everyday. I literally cried myself to sleep at night thinking about the many violations . . . one after another. I cried even more when I thought about the young men who weren't as lucky as me to have college as a way of escape. How could I help them?

Everyday I asked God to take these horrible memories away. Everyday I prayed to God for peace. All of this made me wonder who can you really trust. I was terrified to go to church in college. I came to the conclusion that there are as many traps in the church as there are out in the world. I don't know if I'll ever go to church again, but I know I will never stop praying for those young men who have been and are still being preyed upon rather than prayed for.

Chapter Four

*. . . but why can't I get from two parents
what she can get from one.*

Unlike a lot of my friends, my parents are still married and live under the same roof. They both have pretty decent jobs. We have a nice house in the county. They wear the finest of clothes and give me anything I ask for. I don't think they've ever told me no. Sometimes I don't even get a chance to ask, if they know it's the latest they'll just get it for me. Because of the busyness of their jobs we don't spend a lot of time together. My mom may cook once a week and my dad might make it home in time to have dinner with us, although most times he doesn't. Other than Sundays, when all of our family gets together at my grandparents house for dinner, there is no everybody-sit-at-the-table-at-one-time-and-eat day in our house.

Everybody thinks I'm pretty lucky to have what I have. They see our nice cars. They hear about all that my parents do in the community. They both are quite involved in various community projects and are very respected because of their contributions. My friends hear me mention our annual summer vacation and immediately I am the luckiest kid in the world. What they don't see is that I'm always home by myself. With my mom being a lawyer and my dad a doctor they hardly ever have time for me. It seems like a client or a patient is always put before their own child.

I asked my parents to have another child so that I could have some company, but they laughed at me. They keep telling me to just invite my friends to stay over like that's the answer. I think my parents think if they fill our house and my room with stuff I won't miss them. I think they believe that because I'm 12 years old I don't really need them. When I was younger they were always around. We used to have so much fun. We sat on the floor playing board games. We went to the movies. We were always together . . . the three of us.

I can remember when a night did not go by without my mom or dad kissing me good night. Sometimes I was even lucky enough to have both of them come in to say good night together. Now, my mom yells good night from downstairs, and my dad is almost never home when I go to bed. I try to stay up hoping he'll make it in before I have to go to bed, but my mom makes me go to bed with the assurance that I'll see my dad in the morning.

When I ask my mom to come read to me or something – just to get some of her time and attention – with her head buried in her case file, she says, "You can read to yourself, can't you?" She says, "Sweetie, you're a big girl now." I want to tell her I'm not so big that I don't need some love and attention. But why doesn't she know that already – she's a lawyer. Lawyers are supposed to be smart people.

Last quarter when I got my report card, my friends and I were sharing grades and got all happy about how well we had done. All of us were really excited about going home to tell our parents. One of my friends began to get sad because he said his mother would be too drunk or hung over to even care. My other friend said that her father would fuss about the C, but would probably take her out to celebrate her overall grade average. Another one of my friends said that my parents would probably buy me something big to celebrate my grades, too. I stood there and thought, "If only she knew. I have to find my parents before I can tell them anything. And by the time they get home it won't even be exciting anymore."

When I got home it was just as it always is, no one was there. The house was as lonely and empty as it always is. I then did what I always do, dropped my books and called my mom's office so I could hear her secretary tell me that she was with a client. I asked, as I always did, for her to have my mom call me when she was finished with her client. From there I did what I usually do next. I hung up and paged my dad. There was no sense in calling his office, because he is always out and about seeing his patients or working with his interns. One hour . . . two hours . . . three hours had passed and neither my mom nor my dad had called me back.

In the meantime, my friend called to see if I wanted to go to the mall with her and her father. Her father is a bus drive, but he is always, always there for her. Her mother died two years ago from cancer. She said during the time her mother was dying her father said he would never leave her. That he would always be there for her – no matter what. She said he told her nothing was more important than her, and he meant it. They do everything together, I mean everything. My friend said her father feels more like her best friend than her father. God . . . I wish I knew what that felt like. I'd give anything to know what that feels like. My friend said even when her father disciplines her she doesn't get mad because she knows it's out of love and out of him wanting the best for her.

Like any little girl, I wanted to go to the mall. I appreciated the invitation. But, why can't I get from two parents what she gets from one. That makes me sad, and it makes me feel like my parents don't love me enough to put me first—at least sometimes. I don't understand.

Can my parents' jobs really be that important? Do they not think that parenting me is important? Or maybe they take the fact that I'm a "good little girl" for granted. Maybe if I acted up, got in trouble, or ran away I could get some attention? Maybe the embarrassment of their daughter getting in trouble, or running away (since their status is such a prestigious one) would make them rethink my place in their life. Maybe it would get us into some kind of counseling, and the counselor could tell them they need to be with me more. I don't know! I don't know! I don't know!

Anyway, I went to the mall with my friend and her father, had a great time, and when we got back at 7:00 p.m. my mom was just pulling up in the driveway. She thanked my friend's dad for taking me out with them and then we went in the house. I asked my mother if she got my message from earlier. She said yes but she was too busy to call me back. I checked the messages and my dad had not called me back either. My mom asked me how was school. I wanted to ask her if she really cared, or if she was asking out of habit. About 9:00 p.m. my dad came in. I couldn't get downstairs fast enough to hug him. Even though I don't see my dad a lot, I still get all mooshy when I am lucky enough to see him, especially before going to bed. It's like the biggest treat.

My dad has no idea . . . I really don't think he has any idea what being in his presence does for me. I love my mom, and she's special to me, too. But my dad is like my everything. My granddad said my dad is and has always been very humble and mild mannered. I think my dad is brilliant. The times when we do talk, he tells me stuff that nobody else tells me—not even my teachers in school. I like to read because my dad likes to read. I like the same kind of music my dad likes. I like to hear my dad when he gives speeches. He has a voice like nobody else.

When he has time, and needs what he calls "a moment of peace," he will go for a walk and ask me if I want to go with him. When we go on our walk I wish we never stopped walking. I wish I could lock him into time with me or something, because I never know how long before the next walk. When we walk, we don't talk. He doesn't say anything. Most of the time he has his hands folded behind his back, you can see him thinking, and from time to time he'll look over at me and smile. It doesn't even bother me that he's quiet. I like that he's just there – with his daughter – being my daddy. He always says we can hear God best when we're silent.

They teach us in church that we shouldn't worship anybody else accept God, but I worship my dad. I don't know if it's because I'm still a little girl, or because I never met God in person, but nobody means more to me than my dad.

When I came downstairs and saw my dad I was so happy that I couldn't even be mad anymore. He hugged me and kissed me on the top of my head like he always does. Immediately everything was alright, again. There is something about my dad's hugs and kisses that makes everything alright. I just wish that somehow I could get more of them. My mom probably does too, because she doesn't see him anymore than I do.

I don't care what other people think. I don't care how good the picture looks on the outside. I don't care how much money they make to be able to afford this big house we live in. I would rather have a small house, a little bit of money, and my parents home – any day. This is like the worst life a child could have. I have games, but nobody to play them with. I have good grades, but nobody to appreciate them. I have a big house, but nobody to enjoy it with. I have two parents that I love so much. Two highly educated parents, but they don't have a clue how lonely I am. They don't understand that I need them more than their clients, their patients, and their interns.

Of course I have relatives I can be with. I have friends that would stay every day of the week if I asked them to. But I want my mom and dad. I don't want to be pawned off and shuffled around from house to house because my parents don't have time for me. Why did they have me if they didn't want me? What's the sense in doing good if they don't recognize it? I'm tired of crying myself to sleep. I'm tired of praying to God for my parents to lose their jobs so they can be home.

Sometimes I think I should just kill myself. Then they won't have to bother with me at all. Then they can save their money and stop giving me all this stuff that could never take the place of them. I told my friend that I was thinking about killing myself and she told me she would ask her father to talk to my parents. I told her no because my parents won't listen. I think they think they know everything because they have so many degrees. Although, my dad, because of the type of man he is, he would listen.

I asked my friend if she thought her father would let me come live with them. She said, "Girl, you don't want to live with us. You got all that stuff at your house. You have everything any kid could ask for. We don't even have cable." I told her I didn't care about the stuff or cable. I was just tired of being alone and couldn't take it anymore.

My friend thinks I'm crazy, and a whole lot of other people might think I'm crazy, too, but I would give anything to trade places with her or any kid who's parents pay them some attention. I have to stand in line after the client, the patient, the intern, the community meeting . . . begging and pleading for my parents' attention, and I still don't have as much as I need. My friend, on the other hand, doesn't have to do anything. Her father is just there—all the time.

Chapter Five

*. . . when daddy left did you have
to let him take your dignity and pride out
the door with him?*

It seems like every other week there is a different man. They come in our house, eat our food, sleep in her bed, and then they're gone. I just don't understand what my mother is thinking sometimes.

My mother is a beautiful woman. She has a good job. She's worked hard to get what she has, but she keeps on selling out to these men who mean her no good. And I know they don't mean her any good because of the way they talk to her, and by the way they look at her. They don't love my mother. They just like the fact that she's easy and she don't require nothing of them. What man wouldn't hop on that?

Recently, me and my mother got into this serious argument about me staying out and stuff. She was telling me how ladies carry themselves, and how the girls I was hanging out with weren't good for me. She was basically preaching to me about what's right, and what I should or shouldn't do as a young lady. Why did she go there? I wanted to ask her so bad what qualifies her to tell me anything about right and wrong at this point. Granted she's my mother, and I'll always respect that. But at the same time she needs to be clear that I don't wanna hear what her lips say if she can't back it up with the right actions. Please, she wouldn't take less than my best from me, why should I take less than her best from her.

For the last ten years I have watched my mother's bedroom door slowly turn into a revolving door. I've had to sit at the table and eat with men who were too cheap to even contribute to the dinner, and too lazy to pick their plate up and put it in the sink. I've been watching my younger brother drift further and further away—no doubt because of the men my mother has allowed to treat us any kind of way. They didn't do anything for us. Some of them barely spoke. And somehow that was okay with my mother. How you gonna call yourself digging a guy that doesn't have anything for your kids? Something is wrong with that. I don't have any children, but if I did you better bet the man who wants no parts of my children, wants no parts of me—plain and simple.

I feel so helpless not being able to get my mother to see that she's being played. And my brother, I'm sure that as her son he has to feel absolutely stripped. Sons are supposed to protect their mothers from scum. But what does a son do when his hands have been tied? When he's been sat in a corner, and basically told to mind his business while the mother he loves and wants to protect appears to be throwing her life away; at least a part of her life.

Well, I'll tell you what they do, they find superficial, thankless ways to deal with the inconsistencies that are paraded before them. Then when that doesn't work, they find destructive ways to release the anger and resentment that they have developed as a result of being told – verbally or non-verbally – that what they think doesn't matter.

I watched a vibrant kid turn into a hermit then a terror. It's to a point where my mother can't tell my brother anything. And he ain't tripping off my father either, because he, like me, is still trying to figure out why my father left without warning in the first place. Once upon a time, we had a strong family. We'd sit around and cut up and laugh at my brother's stupid jokes that weren't ever really funny. Me and my mother would team up against my father and my brother in a game of spades. Friday was family night. We took turns choosing how Friday would be spent. It might mean going out to the movies. It might mean going to Blockbusters and getting a movie to watch at home. It might mean going to dinner at a restaurant. Or going bowling, which was one of my favorite picks. Me and my brother would beat my father and mother every time.

But after my father left, when I was seven and my brother was five, nothing has been the same. I don't know if my mother gravitated to multiple men as a way to not deal with she and my father's break up or what. All I know is home is not what it used to be. It no longer feels like our "safe place" because of all the intruders – that's what me and my brother call the supposed-to-be men – that are allowed free reign in our space.

Now, I ain't dumb or insensitive by a long shot. I can only imagine how painful it must be to lose a man you've spent over half your life with. I know that had to hurt my mother, because she was a good wife. Her and my father had what appeared to be a beautiful marriage and a close relationship. It was the coolest thing to see them snugged up on the sofa watching TV, or stretched out across their bed while my mother called herself giving my father a fake massage. He would be laughing so loud we could hear him downstairs. They had so much fun together. Their relationship gave me a sense of what I wanted in a relationship.

So I assume that my mother was as surprised as me and my brother by their separation that eventually turned into a divorce. Even still, my mother stands to gain nothing from handling things the way she's been handling them. Instead she's constantly losing—and she's especially losing the people who are supposed to be dearest to her: her children.

When me and my mother had that blow-up, I wanted so bad to tell her that I'd get my act together when she got her act together, but I knew that would be disrespectful. And despite the fact that she's been disrespecting us and herself, I wasn't about to rub her face in it. She didn't deserve that. So I listened while she lectured, and when she was done I looked her dead in the eyes and respectfully gave her back everything she had given me through the years.

I said, "But mommy, when daddy left did you have to let him take your dignity and your pride out the door with him? Did you have to let him take your hope and your zeal? Mommy, I love you and I appreciate your concern for me, but have you stopped for one minute to think about what kind of affect your choices are having on me and your son? Do you have any idea how difficult it's been for us to just sit back and watch you give yourself away over and over again? For the last ten years that's all you've done?

'Mommy, you and daddy used to be the two people we knew we could go to and get all the right answers. Then, all of a sudden, you stopped. You stopped being our reflection of all that's good and right, and when you did that our attitude became if you don't care why should we care? Mommy, you've been going against everything you ever told us about who we are, and what we should and shouldn't allow. If losing daddy hurts that bad, take some time to deal with the pain. Don't keep running from it, because it's only gonna keep following you like it's been doing. Go talk to somebody. Ask God to help you. You always told us we can ask God for anything. Find a support group for divorced women or something. But for all our sake don't keep trying to find relieve in the arms of men who can't help you. Mommy, they can't even help themselves that's why they're always over here freeloading off of us.

'Mommy, you have always been my role model. You always told us not to settle for less. You always told us to live so that each day got us closer to where we wanted to be. You told us that people would only respect us to the degree we respected ourselves. Now it's like you don't have to practice what you preached. We need our mother back. And mommy, I don't know why you and daddy divorced, but I do know that you can't feel sorry for yourself forever. I know you miss him. We miss him too. We miss seeing yall' together, but mommy, you gotta wanna be alright again. You gotta go inside – like you once told me – and find your strength. You can be that happy, positive woman you were before. You still got it. I believe that . . . do you?"

Although my mother couldn't respond because of the tears that were uncontrollably running down her face, the tight hug she gave me let me know that she knew everything I said was true. I don't think for one second that my mother liked the lifestyle she had been living. I just think it helped to medicate her pain. For me, it's been so amazing to see how pain can rob you, and turn you completely against yourself by turning you into someone else.

My mother's pain took her pretty smile. It took her sense of humor. It took her determination. It took her sense of self worth. But most of all the pain took her focus and her perspective. It really clouded her view—like totally. My mother, the woman before the divorce, would have never even fathomed being promiscuous. Her dignity, what she thought of herself, would not have allowed her to. Yet the very thing she cautioned me against she became.

I cannot tell you the conversations we had as I was growing up where my mother made it crystal clear that I – nobody else – had control over my thoughts, my body, and my destiny. She and my father made me and my brother feel like we were the first and the last of God's best. Our heads were inflated with our parent's belief in us, which is why it's been so devastating watching my mother go through all of this.

We knew that she knew better, because she and our father taught us better. We just didn't know how to get her to see what she was doing to herself and to us. Even though my brother is still out there, I thank God for the chance to speak to my mother on both our behalf. And I thank God that she listened rather than try to shut me up or tell me to stay in a child's place – like adults who are wrong and don't want to hear the truth are famous for doing.

I think one of the saddest things in the world is adults who think they can't learn from children, and as a result always try to silence us or belittle us. My parents always told us that our thoughts were important. My father told us an adult who refuses to listen to a child is an adult who is afraid to know the truth. My mother has helped me through so many things. She's been there with me in good times and in tough times. I can only hope I've been as helpful to her as she's always been to me. Some people say parents and children shouldn't be friends, but me and my mother have always been like the best of friends. As my mother and my friend, I could always count on her. This situation gave me the opportunity to return to her the love and support she's always extended to me.

What would be even more helpful, though, is if I can get my mother and father at least on speaking terms. I think it would make all the difference for my mother. And if the truth be told, my father would be better off, too. I know my father loves my mother, and not even their divorce has taken that love away. Every time I talk to my father he asks how mommy is doing. He always asks if I'm taking good care of her. Why would he ask if he didn't care? If only he wasn't afraid to let her know he still cares?

I just don't understand why divorce has to mean hate? It makes no sense to me that two people spend years and years together, and then all of a sudden they hate each other. I really and truly believe my mother wouldn't have responded to their break up the way she did if she understood that my daddy's leaving wasn't because of anything she did wrong. But, you know, that is what happens when people do not communicate. Everybody is left to think what they wanna think, things get misinterpreted, attitudes flare up, anger kicks in, and then nothing is the same; sort of like it was before I was able to talk to my mother.

Chapter Six

". . . we just didn't think people cared about us "leftovers." That's what some of the workers at the group home called us."

Put me in a group home any day. These so-called foster homes ain't all they're cracked up to be, and the people that call themselves foster parents is a joke. At least in the group home people wasn't in there acting like they loved you. You knew, straight up, they was there to do a job and collect a check. Half of them would tell you straight up they couldn't stand children. But the foster parents who go through classes and stand before a judge and say they want you because they love you and they want to give you of a loving family environment, please. They wouldn't know what love was if it smacked them in the face. For real, I think somebody didn't love them.

I been to three foster homes and only one of them was what they claimed it was gonna be. Them so-called foster parents, most of them anyway, are in it either for the money or to make people think something of them that they ain't. I'm fourteen years old and all my life I been in the foster care system. You might as well say I was born into foster care. I never met neither one of my parents, and at this point I don't even care to. They can let me do my last four years in the group home and then I can make my own way cause far as I'm concerned foster care is a big hustle and I'm tired of being prostituted around.

I know for a fact that some "so-called" foster parents use foster care as a hustle just like drug dealers use drugs for their hustle. It's about getting a new car, or a new house, or new furniture, or home improvements. I'm telling you . . . I actually heard the foster mother at my second foster home talking to somebody on the phone and she was saying how I got on her nerves. She said I was stupid because I couldn't do math that good. She said my social worker must be crazy if he think she gon' go through the trouble of getting me a tutor cause she ain't have time to be picking me up and dropping me off two days a week. She said it probably wouldn't do no good anyway, cause I was messed up from the crack my mother smoked. She said it would be a total waste of time.

The person on the phone must have asked her why she won't help me, and she told them she didn't get me for all that. She said, outta her mouth, that I was her down payment on her new house and the money for her new furniture. She said after her house stuff went through I had to go. I fixed her though. I ran away. I went straight back to my group home, but when they found out where I was they made me go back. I told them I didn't wanna go back because that lady didn't like me or want me. I told them what she said on the phone and everything.

My social worker half believed me. But they believed her more. I think it was because I was only seven years old and most people think that at that age children are only good storytellers. We don't really know what we see or hear; plus she poured it on. She gave up the drama. She acted liked she was really concerned. She even hugged me and kissed me. She told me she missed me. It was a performance and a half. She was so phony. The whole four years I was with her she never hugged me. Seriously, she stayed in her room and I had to stay in my room. I had a nice room with a lot of toys, but I still felt like I was by myself. We didn't talk or play or nothing. A couple times a month we would go somewhere, but I believe that was just for her report. If she wasn't on the phone, she was sleep. I couldn't go outside to play with the other kids, and her house was too pretty for me to roam around. She said she wasn't cleaning up behind nobody else's child.

After I ran away the third time, my social worker let me stay at the group home until they found another foster home. Do you know what it's like wondering where you'll go next, and how the people will treat you when you get there? I hated it. I knew I didn't have a mother or father. I finally got okay with that. I didn't need nobody trying to fill in. I guess it wasn't up to me though, because about eight months later my new social worker—this makes about the sixth different one in fourteen years – came to tell me he had a new family (husband, wife, and two daughters) who was interested in me.

The husband and wife wanted a son but didn't want to try again . . . like that was my problem. Maybe having a man in my life (if he's a real man) might not be that bad a deal. But two girls; what I'm gonna do in a house with two girls. We probably won't have nothing in common. They'll probably get on my nerve. Me being eight, and them being four and eleven already is a problem the way I saw it. Who knows, though, it might work.

And for a while it did. It was straight cool. The third foster home seemed like it was gonna be the place. We had fun. We went places. We sat down for dinner like a real family. I started thinking that maybe I was wrong. Maybe there are people who really can care about children who ain't their own. I finally got so comfortable that I stopped counting down the days and months til I'd be going back to the group home.

One of the things we used to say in the group home was leave before they get rid of you. We used to bet on who'd come back first because we didn't count on people keeping us, and not because we'd do something but because we just didn't think people cared about us "leftovers." That's what some of the workers at the group home called us. It was a trip because you heard it so much that after awhile you saw yourself as just that...a leftover. After a minute, it wasn't a big deal.

Before long what was fun and safe turned into mass confusion. I think the oldest girl got tired of the attention I was getting as the only boy in the "family." Everything was cool for the first two years. The girls called me their brother. My foster mother and father called me their son, and told me to call them mommy and daddy, which almost never happens. It was the third and final year that things fell apart, and to this day I don't know what that something was.

One day my foster mother and father came to my room and said they needed to talk to me. They had these serious looks on their faces like I never saw before from them. Soon as they shut the door, I asked them if everything was okay, and they said that's what they came to ask me. I was lost. I didn't know what they meant. I hadn't done no wrong.

I mean I was scared to mess up, cause they was so good to me. I really liked them. I would be stupid to blow this—and I didn't. But according to my foster mother and father the oldest girl said that I told her and her little sister that I was gonna do some inappropriate things to them one day while we was down the basement. I couldn't believe it. I was mad. I told my foster mother and father that I would never do nothing like that. I told them I couldn't image why their daughter would even say something like that.

Instantly, though, I got this feeling in my throat. I knew I was on the clock...time was winding up. I knew what the deal was, cause I knew the feeling...I felt it before. It was one thing different, though. This time, I knew my foster mother and father loved me and really cared about me. Them loving me still didn't remove the fact that if it came down to choosing sides, I'd lose—hands down. I knew that, for whatever reason, the oldest girl was setting me up . . . big time.

This was her domain, and I...some kinda way...I had become some annoying intruder, instead of the big brother she was so happy to have when I first got there. Never mind I hadn't done nothing but be myself. I hadn't switched up or nothing. But to keep things where I couldn't be suspect or accused of anything else, I just stayed away from her completely. I tried not to be no where near her unless somebody else was around. Cause for real, this was a good thing, and I wasn't trying to mess it up.

She was slick, though . . . real slick. Wherever I was in the house, the oldest girl would follow me. She was all playful and joking and always up in my face like she was cool or something. But I wasn't trying to get caught in her trick bag. I wasn't trying to be fooled by her or her smoke screen. I knew, straight up, she wasn't to be trusted. A little over three months later she did it again. This time, though, she told my foster mother and father that I showed her and her little sister my private part. This time I wasn't mad, I was furious. I was burning up. I couldn't believe how hard this girl was working to do me in. I ain't never been this good in all my ten and a half years, but what did it get me. I told my foster mother and father who was real upset about all this that I appreciated all they'd done to make me feel a part of their family, but I'd just rather go back to the group home. I told them I didn't know what was up with their daughter. I just knew she was lying on me—deep. I told them all I could think was that she probably didn't want me there no more and she was trying to give them a reason to put me out. And you know what, they believed me.

Later on that day all five of us came together in the living room to talk about things, and the oldest girl couldn't look nobody in the face while she told her lies of how stuff supposedly happened. The youngest girl never said nothing, and when her mother and father asked her stuff she looked at her sister. It was crazy. And it didn't take long before even their mother and father knew they both was lying.

After the talk my foster mother and father told the girls to go to their room, and me and my foster father went for a walk. He told me how much he loved me, and how he enjoyed having me for a son. He said he appreciated the changes he saw in me. It felt like a good-bye speech. But then he said he was gonna work on his daughters. He told me not to worry about things . . . that everything was gonna be fine. I heard him, but because I knew how this stuff usually played out, I couldn't chance it. I'm the leftover, remember, which means if anybody is gonna be thrown out, it's gonna be me.

With no other choice I took to the golden rule. I left before they could put me out. This time, though, I went to my social worker's office. He was cool. I liked him better than any of my other workers, and I wanted him to know—from me first—how things went down. He was with somebody so I had to wait for almost two hours. By time I saw him the people had already called to say I was gone. I told him there was no way I was gonna go back there because that oldest girl was trying to put a charge on me. I know the system. I wasn't goin' out like that. It wasn't worth it.

My social worker was mad cause he knew how hard I was trying. Even my foster mother and father was mad, especially my foster father, because we did everything a father and son could do. He liked me being there just as much as I liked being there. He actually wanted me to come back. He talked to me. He talked to my social worker. And, I did wanna go back, but then I didn't wanna go back.

I wanted to go back because I wanted to be with my foster mother and father, and even the youngest girl cause she was real cool. But then I didn't wanna go back because that oldest girl was wicked. She was on another sheet of music than the rest of us. Her tune was entirely different than ours…for real. She had issues like us foster system kids, and she hadn't even been in the system. What's up with that? I would think that kids who had two parents – especially parents that was as nice as hers – would have a better head on their shoulder.

Kids like me, thought, the world expect that we crazy. They expect us to do dumb, stupid stuff. We supposedly got *acceptable* excuses or *valid* reasons for why we act like we do. Anyway, my social worker agreed with me and told my foster mother and father that their house was "too hostile an environment," and therefore not safe for me anymore. He told them that it was in my best interest, and in the best interest of their daughters that he find me another placement.

Why? How? What went wrong? I don't know. I just know I'm back where I started (nowhere) for the millioneth time. Now I can really understand that saying people say: *Sometimes even your best ain't good enough.*

AFTERWARD FOR ADULTS

You have read. You have heard. Now what? What have you to say? What will you do? What can our youth expect from you? What part have you played in preventing or contributing to their pain? What will it take to convince you that our youth are in need of your investment?

As compelling and as heart wrenching as each of these stories are I employ you to not be caught up in a momentary whirlwind of emotionalism. Because as fate would have it, the whirlwind of emotionalism like any other whirlwind will see its calm. You and I, on the other hand, cannot afford to calm down as we purpose to give our young people the attention, nurturing, and support their hungry souls so desperately crave. Our interest must be under girded by unconditional love, and sustained by unwavering commitment. Our expectations of and belief in our young people must be such that they feel and become that which we expect and believe. Anything else is sure to become like that of moisture: it's there, it evaporates, and eventually it is no more.

There are no two ways about it, our youth need us. Right now . . . today, and every day. They need us listening to them. They need us investing in them. They need us fighting for them – intentionally and relentlessly. Their cause must be our business. Their needs must be our concern. Healing their hurt and reconciling their pain must be our motivation.

As illustrated in the stories, every young person had an adult or some adults around them. The question becomes in what capacity were the adults around them. Were the adults helpful, encouraging, available, engaging, and loving? Some were, and unfortunately, some were not. Inasmuch as we may be able to differ in opinion with respect to the roles the adults played, or the capacity in which they served, what is indisputable is the impact of the adults' presence in the lives of the youth. There was indeed an impact – be it positive or negative.

It is incumbent upon us, therefore, to make certain that we are not simply *present* in our young peoples' lives. Our presence has to be so positively prevailing that it invokes life, transforms thinking, answers prayers, downright destroys hopelessness, and causes our young people to hold themselves up to a standard of living that's nothing short of excellence.

When we look at the tall order of the task before us (and it is a tall order) we would quickly contend that we have our work cut out for us. We would also venture to say that the drudgery of trying to keep a flame ignited that is constantly being blown out by others' carelessness and disregard is seemingly more challenging than it is worth. But what's truer and deeper than either of these things is the reward. Planting the seeds. Having the patience to penetrate through all the emotional baggage. Seeing the actual manifestation of the change. Knowing you were instrumental, and to some degree, responsible for the transformation of a young person's wayward thinking.

Hear me when I tell you there is nothing more beneficial. There is nothing more reassuring than being privileged to see the fruits of your labor. There is nothing more fulfilling than seeing a young person come to the conclusion that they are somebody when for years they thought they were nobody – all because of *your* investment. All because you felt it not robbery to open your heart and extend yourself. All because you did more than talk, gossip, and/or complain; you aligned yourself with our young peoples' needs.

When you put this book down and walk away from it, I can only hope that you will not walk away from its call or from its charge. Rather, I pray that you will find your way to a young person, or some young people. It could even be your own offspring. Put your arms around them. Touch them. Affirm their worth. Speak life to them. Tell them what that person who made a difference in your life told you. Give them something to hold on to when they are sitting in the cafeteria at school wondering why no one will sit with or by them.

Or when when they've messed up so bad that they have convinced themselves there is no getting up. Or they've done everything right but somehow everything keeps going all wrong, and in the midnight hour with tears running down their face the only two words they can utter are, "Why me?" Above all, tell them that you love them and make certain the proclamation is backed up with demonstration that's real and substantive. You will not regret it—not for one moment. I guarantee you won't.

AFTERWARD FOR YOUTH

Some would have you as a young person believe that adults always make the best decisions thus the right decisions. In fact, in the short time that you have been here on this earth some adult has probably already said to you, "I've lived a lot longer than you therefore I believe I know a lot more than you do."

While it is the case that age *can* equate to increased knowledge and/or wisdom, it is not the case that this is always true. Quite frankly, in too many instances it is sadly not true. As a result, all over the world we have young peoples' lives – like the young people you just read about in this book – that have been negatively affected or influenced by adults who ended up not being the best examples. We have young people who have been psychologically, mentally, and emotionally traumatized by an adult they thought they could trust. And while that adult continues on with his/her life, he/she leaves behind a young person who has been placed in the awkward position of having to work through their pain, betrayal, disappointment, and anger the best way they know how to.

Whether you are a young person that fits into either of the categories above or not, what I want you to know is that you…and you alone have ultimate power over your thinking, your choices, and your behavior. I want you to know that regardless of the influences around you, it is your job to go within yourself and commit to learning how to be the best person you can be. Although it may be somewhat uncomfortable; although it may be somewhat difficult to learn how to do something you have never done before, I want you to know that I am confident you can find your way to your best self.

Now, does this mean that you have to do it alone? No. Does this mean that you should expect instant results? No. Does this mean that letting go, forgiving, and leaving the past behind will be easy? No. What it does mean, though, is in the face of whatever you may be challenged by you no longer have to allow *that thing* or *that situation* or *that person* to continually define you and/or hold you back from making positive, productive decisions that will ultimately turn your life in the direction of success.

Hear me when I tell you that young people like adults must not allow excuses of any kind to become a reason for not coming into the knowledge of how great your potential truly is. And I know this is true, because as a teenager I made a complete mess of my life. I hung around all the wrong people and I always made reckless decisions. As a result, I was stuck in this constant cycle of nothingness. That is until I met these two amazing women who believed things about me that I finally began to believe about myself. As change happened for me so can it happen for you; you simply have to want it bad enough.

YOUTH SERVING ORGANIZATIONS

LOCAL ORGANIZATIONS

BALTIMORE RISING
www.baltimorecity.gov

URBAN LEADERSHIP INSTITUTE
www.urbanleadershipinstitute.com

INTERNATIONAL YOUTH FOUNDATION
www.iyfnet.org

MARYLAND MENTORING PARTNERSHIP
www.marylandmentors.org

COALITION OF COMMUNITY FOUNDATIONS FOR YOUTH
www.ccyf.org

THE AFTER SCHOOL INSTITUTE
www.afterschoolinstitute.org

JOHNS HOPKINS BLOOMBERG SCHOOL OF PUBLIC HEALTH
CENTER FOR THE PREVENTION OF YOUTH VIOLENCE
www.jhsph.edu/PreventYouthViolence/Resources/maryland.resources.html

NATIONAL ORGANIZATIONS

Help Your Community.org
www.helpyourcommunity.org

Children's Defense Fund
www.childrensdefense.org

Teen-Rescue.org
www.teen-rescue.org

National Youth Coalition
www.nyacyouth.org

Boys & Girls Club of America
www.bgca.org

Advocates for Youth
www.advocatesforyouth.org

Youth Build Academy for Transformation
www.youthbuild.org

National Youth Development Information Center
www.nydic.org

National 4-H Youth Development Program
www.4-H.org

NOTE: In most cases when you visit a national website you can locate your local chapter or branch by putting in your city, state, and/or zip code.

ORDERING INFORMATION

Name: _____

Address: _____

_____

City, State, Zip: _____

_____

_____Copies @ $10.00 + S&H = _____

Please send check/money order in the amount of $10.00 plus
$2.50 per book to: 2327 Harlem Avenue, Baltimore, Maryland
21216. Make checks payable to: Mischa P. Green.

For more information about our company, Greatness Now!, our
trainings, products, and other publications visit us online at
www.greatnessnow.org. Please also feel free to e-mail us your
comments and feedback at greatnessnow@hotmail.com.

OTHER BOOKS BY MISCHA P. GREEN

Sacred: 100 Affirmations for Girls

Revolutionary Revelations

What Tough Times Tough Me

30 Things He Told Me But Can't Tell You Because You Won't Listen